Holy Manna

Happy and Tracey Chirara

Parson's Porch Books

Holy Manna
ISBN: Softcover 978-1-955581-78-3
Copyright © 2022 by Happy and Tracey Chirara

Parson's Porch Books is an imprint of Parson's Porch *and* Company (PP&C) in Cleveland, Tennessee. PP&C is an innovative organization which raises money by publishing books of noted authors, representing all genres. Its face and voice is **David Russell Tullock.** *dtullock@parsonsporch.com.*

Parson's Porch *and* Company *turns books into bread and milk* by sharing its profits with the poor.

www.parsonsporch.com

Holy Manna

Contents

Pursue your Original Goal at Whatever Cost

Genesis 29:21-28: Philippians 4:13

Jacob loved Rachel from the beginning, and he was prepared to do everything to get her. He would not allow any obstacle to stand in his way or block him from pursuing Rachel. Many people today are failing to pursue their dreams because of disappointments. Others are given substitutes. We are told that Jacob was promised by Laban that after working for 7 years he would receive Rachel as his bride but after the wedding night Jacob found out that he was given a substitute/Leah and not the desire of his heart Rachel. A substitute is not your first choice this is why in football you will see all the substitutes sitting on a bench, waiting for emergencies. Rachel was Jacob's first choice, but he was given Leah a substitute. What would your reaction be like when the world gives you substitutes? Some of us have been diverted from our goals because of substitutes. Others have been contented by Leah a substitute, but i like Jacob's attitude, 'Leah is not my goal, I will pursue my Rachel.' Friends in Christ, before you receive the desires of your heart sometimes life gives you a substitute or a disappointment. Life may give you what you don't want. You might be a qualified teacher, nurse, Accountant, an Engineer, Lawyer, etc but life has given you something else/ a substitute or a Leah instead of your Rachel and you are now contented with that substitute. Heeeeeey! Never be contented with Leah, she is not your portion, but pursue your goal.

What do you do when life gives you a Leah instead of Rachel, what do you do when those whom you trusted betray you, what do you do when you are given a substitute or when you encounter some disappointments on your way to your goal and what will be your reaction when you expected a big yes and life gives you a big no? Look at Jacob, He was determined to pursue his Rachel come hail come thunder. Jacob never gave up; he accepted the situation, but he said i will still pursue my Rachel. I will go after my dream and goal. I will not settle for less because I am destined for greater things. This year refuse to settle for substitutes/Leah but pursue your original dream, goal in Jesus name. Leah is not my portion, i will go after what i wanted first. Don't give in to those disappointments standing in your way to your goal but pursue your goal, dream or the desires of your life. Put the Leah behind you and pursue your Rachel. I declare that this year i will not find rest until i get hold of my goal and i will not allow Leah to shift my focus from Rachel. There is a goal to attain and a victory to be won, give me power every hour to victory.. Pursue your original goal or dream and never allow substitutes to divert your attention. Paul in Philippians 4:13 says, 'I can do everything through Christ who gives me strength.' With Christ on your side no disappointment or substitute will divert you from your original goal and you will not settle for substitutes or lesser things, but you will settle for greater things in life. Pursue your Rachel at whatever cost.

With Christ the Devil's Furnace Becomes a Catalyst to Your Greatness

Daniel 3:25-26,30

The above story tells us of 3 friends who demonstrated their faith and refused to worship any other gods except Yahweh. These friends would not compromise their faith and they were thrown into the fiery furnace. The King ordered that the fire be 7 times more than the usual fire. Instead of being consumed by the fire, they found a friend, Jesus the fire neutralizer and fire Quencher in the furnace. What a friend we have in Jesus? He is a friend in the furnace, a friend in the valley of the shadow of death, a friend in the lion's den, and His name is Jesus The Fire Quencher and Fire Neutralizer. Jesus came not to make life Easy but to make People great in the presence of the devil and his furnaces. Brothers and Sisters in Christ, you need to pass through the furnace on your way to greatness. Don't try to avoid their furnaces, let them prepare their fire, and those furnaces will be catalysts to your greatness.

The Bible says, Nebuchadnezzar after throwing these three friends in the furnace said, "Look i saw four men walking around in the fire, unbound and unharmed, and the fourth man looks like a son of the gods." Note that the owner of the furnace saw people walking freely and unharmed in his fire accompanied by the fire Neutralizer. Friends you need to pass through your enemies fire for you to emerge out stronger, greater, better and purer. The bible in verse 26 says, Nebuchadnezzar begged the 3 boys to get out of his furnace. With Christ on your side, your enemies are going to beg you to get out of their furnaces which were meant to consume you to ashes. This time you will get out of the devil's furnace with promotions attached.

Daniel 3:30 says, "Then the King promoted Shadrach, Meshach and Abednego in the province of Babylon." With Christ on our side the devil's furnace will act as a catalyst to our greatness, to our promotion, to our elevation in Jesus name. We love this Jesus who is a friend even in the devil's furnaces. So worry not when your enemies are busy throwing you in their furnaces, because this time Jesus is gonna change all the devil's furnaces to be our catalysts to our greatness. Instead of being consumed by their fire, we will be promoted in their furnace. Face that furnace meant to torture your marriage, health, relationship, your children etc with steadfastness and you will emerge out of that furnace with greatness and promotions attached to your life in Jesus name. With Christ the devil's furnace will be turned to be a catalyst to our greatness and all the devil's furnaces meant to consume us, our marriages, jobs, businesses etc to death will be quenched and Neutralized in Jesus name. Jesus Christ came not to make life easy but to make us great in the presence of our enemies and their furnaces. With Christ the devil's furnaces will become vehicles or catalysts to our promotion and greatness.

With Christ No Worldly Pressure Will Break Us

2 Corinthians 4:8

In the above text Paul describes this Christian life, in which infirmity is intermingled with God's glory. Verse 8 says, "we are so pressed at every point but not crushed; perplexed but not in despair." This statement means that worldly pressures in this life can make us reach the breaking or bursting points but with Christ we will not burst or break. Of course our lives are surrounded by various forms of pressures. We are hard pressed by family pressures, employment pressures, marriage pressures, political pressures, financial pressures, pressures coming from our churchmates, children, in laws, evil spirits, witches, satanists, etc. We are hard pressed, and we have reached the breaking point and we are about to break. Life is full of pressures, but we are never in so tight a corner that there is no way out. Poverty, sour marriages, barrenness, miscarriages, unsound health, witches, etc can press us to the bursting point, but this time we refuse to break. This year we shall encounter a lot of pressure from all corners or all angles but pray for the resilient power so that you can be pressed or stretched to the breaking point, but you will refuse to break. Pray for the power to be resilient like a tennis ball no matter how strong your hands are you cannot press it and break it. Of course, it can reach the bursting or breaking point, but it will never break or burst.

Friends in Christ, you are under pressure and you are feeling it in your spirit that you have reached the breaking point and you are about to break, listen to us and listen good, with Christ you can reach the breaking point and not break, you can reach the bursting point and not burst and there is always a way out. No matter how strong the hands pressing you are, worry not you will not break or burst. With Christ we are given the resilientnt power and there is always an element of spaciousness in you. Fear not those who are busy pressing your life, marriage, health, relationship, spouse, finances, business, Ministry, etc, believe in Christ and you will refuse to break. With Christ No worldly pressure can make our life, marriages, etc break, no matter how big it is. As we are pursuing our goals, there are some pressures which we will encounter but focus on Christ and you will receive the resilient power. This time we can reach the breaking or bursting point, but we refuse to break in Jesus name. Of course the devil and his/her agents are busy piling pressure on my marriage, relationship, my health, projects, education, career, etc and they are about to break them, this time we will not break or burst in Jesus name. Stretch me to the breaking point but I will not break, press me to the bursting point but i will not burst. With Christ no worldly pressure can break us. We pray for the resilient power to be our portion as we are facing various pressures being piled against us by our enemies and those who are jealous about our lives, our success or our good marriages, our excellence at work, in Ministry at school, etc. Claim the resilient power and you can reach the breaking point and not break.

With Christ You Can Be Knocked Down But Not Knocked Out

2 Corinthians 4:9

In the above text, Paul is aware that if a person would share the life of Christ he/she must share the risks of Christ. To be a strong Christian doesn't mean that you will not fall, but that every time you fall you will rise again. Paul says, "...we are knocked down but not knocked out." This means that to be knocked down is not to be knocked out of the game, to be beaten doesn't mean ultimate defeat, losing a battle is not losing the campaign. Friends in Christ, life is full of challenges, evil spirits whose major agenda is to knock us down both physically and spiritually. You have been knocked down by the devil at your workplace, in your marriage, in your business, relationship, at your school, in your family, Church etc and the devil is having an upper hand over your life. Of course you have been beaten and you are down spiritually, and your enemies are busy celebrating your fall. You have been beaten and knocked down by poverty, inflation, misfortunes, sickness, rejection, sour marriage, barrenness, spirit of stagnation or anti progress demons, unjustified wars and your enemies are busy celebrating your downfall at school, in business, in marriage, at work, in Ministry, in politics etc. My friend listen to me and listen well, to be knocked down is not to be knocked out of the game, to be beaten doesn't mean ultimate defeat and losing a battle doesn't mean losing the campaign.

I like a Wrestler by the name The Undertaker or the dead Man. Sometimes He can be beaten to the point that He would ly flat in the middle of the ring like a dead person but that doesn't mean that The Undertaker will lose the game. Despite being beaten to the point of death The Undertaker would end up being the Winner and He won more than 20 consecutive WrestleMania games. Friends, with Christ on your side you can be beaten to the point of death, but you will refuse ultimate defeat, you can be knocked down, but you will refuse to be knocked out of the ring, you may lose the battle, but you will refuse to lose the campaign. Are you feeling defeated, knocked down? Are your enemies and opponents appearing to be having an upper hand over you? Brethren, be encouraged by the above words of Paul, with Christ, we are knocked down but not out. Nothing here on earth can knock us out of the game, kudonhedzwa hakuziri ku loser campaign. Even if the devil comes like a flood, i refuse to be knocked out of the game. This 2019 refuse to be knocked out of your marriage, refuse the devil to knock you out of your business, relationship, project, career, education, etc in Jesus name.

Fit into God's Calendar and You Will Know that God's Time is Always Sweet

Habakkuk 2:3

People have their own calendars of events. A calendar is a planned program of events with fixed time. It's good to plan and have your own life calendar but one has to be aware of the fact that God has his own calendar and God's calendar supersedes our own personal calendars. His calendar and our calendar may differ on time, but one thing for sure is that God means what He says, although there might be delays. God operates in His own schedule, that is why in Habakkuk 2:3 He says, "but things i plan won't happen right away. Slowly, steadily, surely, the time approaches when the vision will be fulfilled." If it seems slow, don't despair for these things will surely come to pass. They will not be overdue a single day. Friends Delay is not denial, so when things seem to be taking long don't lose heart, never give up but know that God has his own calendar which sometimes differs from our own calendars, but God's time is always sweet. In most cases we get tired of delays, and we often botch things up and like

Abraham and Sarah we are quick to create our own Ishmaels instead of waiting for our Isaac.

How many Ishmaels have we created out of desperation? It is the waiting period that makes us to be stuck and jump right into the middle of trouble. Delay is not denial, so wait patiently and don't create your Ishmael because God is going to bring you your Isaac. Be like Hannah who waited patiently for her Samuel. Fit into God's calendar and you will realize that God's time is always sweet. Your Samuel is coming but you need to fit into God's calendar before you to realize your rightful portion. You have been waiting for your marriage, wedding, good job, career, good health, successful business, etc for quite a longtime now. You have been delayed in completing your education, acquiring a residential stand, a house, vehicle, to conceive, etc and you are now hopeless and about to quit. According to our own human calendar you are out of time, and everything appears to be Hannah's dead or barren womb, but according to God's own calendar you are still in time and out of that dead and barren womb your Samuel shall come forth. God operates on His own schedule and slowly, steadily, surely, the time approaches when the vision will be fulfilled. So fit into God's calendar and you will receive your rightful portion. If you fit yourself into other people's calendars , you will stress yourself or commit suicide, but you need to fit into God's plan and definitely you will receive your Samuel. Never lose hope but fit into God's plan and it shall be well, and you will know that God's time is always sweet.

The Darker the Shadow the Closer
The Lord

Psalms 23:4

The above text is a Psalm written by David out of his own sour experiences he encountered as a Shepherd, from Goliath, Saul and from his family. The word shadow can mean a substance or one who secretly or furtively follows another. A shadow is merely a hint of the real substance. It's a dark image projected onto a surface where light is blocked.[1] So when David is saying, 'even though i walk through the valley of the shadow of death, i will fear not because my Shepherd is with me... His rod and staff will comfort me' (Psalms 23:4), He is saying that even though I walk through an elongated depression where a dark image is projected against my life so as to block the light and where some people, evil spirits etc are secretly and furtively following or trekking my life, i will fear not, because the good Shepherd is by my side. The darker the shadow or the more frightening is the shadow the more closer is my Jesus. We have seen that a shadow is a dark image projected against something whose job is to block light, thus a shadow is associated with darkness. In life we are passing through these valleys characterized by the shadows of death or darkness and stalkers. It might be your health, marriage, relationship, business, career, job, Ministry etc which is passing through a dark valley where your enemies are following or trekking you secretly. The shadow is getting darker day by day and you are about to lose your life, children, spouse, job, business, relationship etc. We want to remind you that with Jesus the good Shepherd on your side no amount of darkness cast by those shadow will overcome God's light because the darker the shadow the closer is our Jesus.

Moreso a shadow is just a hint of the real substance but it's not the real substance. The shadow of divorce is just a hint of divorce but it's not the real divorce, so fear not that shadow of death secretly following your life, marriage, career, education, project etc, it's just a shadow and not the real death. The darker the shadow the closer the Lord. So fear not all the shadows of death casting darkness in your life, marriage, future, children, poultry, piggery, hairdressing, sewing, cross-border trading projects etc, with Christ you will walk or pass through that valley or elongated depression of darkness safely because the darker the shadow, the closer the Lord. Even if your health is passing through the shadow of death and your enemies are secretly following and monitoring your life, worry not because the darker the shadow, the closer the Lord and His rod and Staff will protect you as you will be walking through all the elongated depressions full of darkness and stalkers who are secretly following our lives day in day out. With Christ the good shepherd on our side, no shadow will block the light of Christ from reaching us and no witch, satanist, enemy, evil spirit will secretly follow us and succeed. Friends fear not all those valleys of the shadows of death following your life, family etc, they are just hints and not the real object. It's just a shadow of death and not the real death. Fear not all that darkness casted against your life by that shadow which is secretly following your life, take Jesus as your Shepherd this year and you will realize that it's just a shadow of death and not the actual death. You will also realize that the more darker the shadow is the more closer is my Jesus with his rod and staff. The Darker the shadow, the more Closer is my Jesus.

People Bury but God Plants

Genesis 37:8-24; 41:38-45

The devil and his agents use pits to bury your talent, health, your intelligence, life, potential, children etc but our God uses the very same pits to plant a person into a giant. In the above texts, Joseph's brothers were too jealous of Joseph's gift of dreaming, and they hated him to the extent of planning to eliminate him from the scene. Brothers and sisters in Christ, we are living in a world where our good deeds and talents can invite hatred from our colleagues in ministry, at work, school, in business, communities, families etc. Instead of cultivating their brother's gift of dreaming, Joseph's brothers hated him to death, and they agreed to throw Joseph into a deep pit. People bury but God plants. 'Here comes the Dreamer, let's throw him in the pit.' Joseph's gift of dreaming was meant to save the whole family in the coming severe hunger, but his brothers saw it as a threat, and they decided to bury and eliminate that which was to save them in the near future. Joseph found himself in a pit, but God was planting him to be a Prime Minister. Friends worry not when your rivals, relatives, enemies, colleagues etc are pitting your life, job, marriage, health, relationship, business etc in their pits. Joseph's brothers were determined to burry and eliminate him from the scene, but God used their instruments of cruelty to work for Joseph's own good and to produce positive results.

Our enemies can try to make life very difficult for me and rejoice as we suffer but they will be ashamed one day to see us rising and shining from their pit. Believe in the God who changes the devil's pits to be conducive environments for our germination. Of course your enemies and rivals have pitted/ buried your career, project, health, future, fertility, peace, spouse, children, talent, etc, they have pulled you down to the bottom of their pits and they are now busy celebrating and feasting on the fruits of your labour thinking that you are now history. The bible tells us that, after throwing Joseph into the pit his brother sat down to eat the food brought by Joseph. They only wanted Joseph's food. That's the human nature. Human beings want your food or benefits only. You have been pulled down and buried, all your hopes to rise up and progress in business, at work, in school, etc have been shattered, in such a situation, Worry not my friend, but believe in a God who used your enemy's instrument of destruction for your own good. This year God is gonna use all your enemies pits meant to bury your life, multiplication, marriage, relationship, health, excellence, etc as fertile grounds to plant you and make you grow into a giant. Fear not my friend when your enemies have finished burying your life and your possessions in their pits, our God is going to use the very same pits to plant your life so that it will grow into a giant in that pit. People bury but God plants.

When your Season Comes Nothing Will Stop You

Psalms 30:5

The word season means a fit or suitable time; the convenient time; usual or appointed time.[2] Thus to be in season means to be in good, suitable or sufficiently early for the purpose and to be out of season means to be late, beyond the proper time. In the above text the Psalmist is saying, 'weeping may stay for a night, but joy comes in the morning."(Psalms 30:3) Night is the period of darkness, confusion, chaos, stagnation, no meaningful progress, unfruitfulness, etc but one interesting thing is that no darkness has the power to stop the sun from rising. The darkest hour of the night is the period just before dawn. Friends in Christ night or darkness may come in your life, family, nation, etc but remember that no darkness has the power to stop the sun from rising. No matter how dark the night is, no darkness has the power to stop the sun from rising. When your season comes nothing will stand in your way. Everyone has his/her season so don't be jealous when you see others being married, getting good jobs, prospering in their farms, flea markets, vegetable markets, projects, booming in business, buying stands or building houses, buying cars, excelling in Ministry or in school etc and you are stuck or trapped and unable to move or progress. They are in their season, and your season shall come also. A guava tree doesn't worry when the lemon tree is producing fruits in its season, so wait for your own season. Of course the night and its darkness come into your life, marriage, health, education, business, Church etc with its dark moments, pain, confusion, frightening experiences, sour experiences, stagnant and unfruitful experiences etc, but worry not my friend, weeping may stay just for a night but soon and very soon the darkness will give way to the morning light.

No matter how dark your situation is, darkness will not stand in the way of the morning light and succeed. So wait for your appointed time, your season shall come, and nothing will stop it from coming your way. Are you weeping for your job, your marriage, relationship, your children, brothers or sisters, your health, finances, church, family, nation, your farm etc? Be assured that your season shall come, and nothing will stop it from coming. When you see me sitting in Nandoos or chicken inn without food on my table don't feel pity for me, i am waiting for my special order. Special orders took time to be prepared. Pizza took time to be prepared unlike steak pies. So don't feel pity for me when you see me sitting there without anything on my table i am waiting for my Pizza to come at the appropriate time. When you see me without a good salary, a stand, a family, etc don't feel pity for me, Ii am waiting for my special order and my season is coming. When my season comes nothing will stand in my way. Weeping may stay for a night but one thing for sure is that joy comes in the morning . With Christ on my side no amount of darkness will block my morning light from coming my way. Its weeping time but your season to excel, get a sound marriage, sound relationship, true joy, peace, a good paying job, to fruitful in everything, to be promoted, to extend and enlarge your territory, to be Compensated is coming and nothing will stop it. Remain focused on Christ during these dark hours and wait patiently for your right time. Weeping may come in the night, but joy comes in the morning. Your season shall come and all that darkness covering your life shall give way to the morning light in Jesus name.

Be the Hot Stone of Your Family

2 Samuel 21:10-14

The name Rizpah means a Hot stone. In the above text we are told that King David took two sons of Rizpah and delivered them in the hands of the Gibeonites as compensation for the sins committed by their father Saul. The Gibeonites hanged them in the hill and were killed in the harvest season. Then Rizpah took sackcloth, and spread it for her upon the rock, from the beginning of harvest until water dropped upon them out of heaven, and she could not allow neither the birds of the air to devour his sons' bodies by day nor the beasts of the field by night. Be the Hot stone of your family and never allow the vultures targeting your life, family, children, etc to devour your portion. Note that Rizpah spread a cloth on a rock, and she sat on top of a rock. Jesus is the rock ages and with Him on your side you will become a hot stone, and you will fight to the finish.

Of course the devil has captured and hanged your children, spirit, life, spouse, relative, marriage, relationship, job, business, mind, etc and the devil is appearing to be on the winning side and is now relaxing thinking that the game is over. They hanged your only source of hope. I like the Rizpah or Hot stone spirit, the spirit that will not allow the vultures and beasts of this world to devour and feast on our children, families, spouses, possessions, etc. Be the Hot stone of your family and you will command all the vulture spirits to flee from your life and family. Be the Hot stone and fight for your children, fight for your marriage, fight for your spirit, fight for your relationship, fight for your career and never allow the vultures of your enemies to devour your portion in Jesus name. Be the Rizpah of your generation and fight for your generation. It's better to lose the comfort of a nice home defending your family, children, marriage, job, education, relationship, etc than to enjoy a luxurious life while vultures are feasting on your character, integrity, spirit, mind, children, spouse, marriage etc. Be the Hot stone of your family and no vulture will devour your portion. You need to stand on Jesus the rock of ages for you to be the Rizpah/Hot stone of your family. With Christ on your side you will not give up the fight, you will sacrifice even your body and time and you will fight to the finish.

Reject the Grasshopper Mentality and Claim the Conquering Spirit

Numbers 13 25-33

The above text tells us about Moses instructing his people to go and spy the promised land. 12 spies, one from each tribe of Israel were send and they did the spying and came back with two contradicting reports concerning the Giants or Anakites. The Bible tells us that they all agreed that the land was good, and they brought the fruits of that land as evidence that indeed it was a fertile land, but they differed on the issue of their capacity to go and take back their land of promise from the Anakites. Ten out of 12 spies said we can't go and face the Anakites because they are giants, and we were like grasshoppers to them. Their mindsets made them to see themselves as grasshoppers. Friends in Christ, grasshopper mentality is very dangerous and if you are a victim of this grasshopper mentality you will not advance to your promise or you will not adventure. The grasshopper mentality in this case refers to the spirit which will make a person feel inferior, feel useless, defeated even before the battle. This spirit has made some of us to fail to achieve in life, to miss opportunities, to just sit and look at the enemy feasting on our portion.

Of course the Anakites where giants but the Israelites were the rightful owners of the land. The ten spies with the grasshopper mentality suggested that it was better to leave the Anakites feasting on their land of promise than to attempt to face them and repossess their stolen property. They forgot that they were a chosen generation, and they were God's children/ Yahweh the Mighty Warrior. The grasshopper mentality overshadowed their minds to the extent that they failed to see the greatness of their God. Then comes Caleb and Joshua, these two spies trusted their God so much that they rejected the grasshopper mentality, and they claimed the spirit of a Giant. Their story was, 'of course the Anakites are giants and are there but let's go and take back what is rightfully ours and definitely we will conquer.

Today we want to claim this victorious spirit and command that grasshopper mentality in us to flee in Jesus name. Declare that I am not a grasshopper, but I am a Giant. You have been looking down upon yourself at your school, workplace, in business, family, Church, etc, be optimistic and you will restore all your stolen property. Don't just sit and watch the devil tormenting, feasting on your children, spouse, health, etc but reject the grasshopper mentality and claim the Conquering spirit and you will definitely conquer in Jesus name. Believe in the risen Christ and that grasshopper mentality hovering around your life, marriage, children etc will flee for good in Jesus name. This is your year of refusing to be a victim of the grasshopper mentality in your Church, at your school, workplace, in your family etc in Jesus name. Of course the giants of the enemy have grabbed your land of promise and they are busy feasting on your rightful portion. Claim the victorious spirit to be your portion and never allow the grasshopper mentality to take charge of your life. Believe in Christ and you will reject that grasshopper mentality in Jesus name.

The God Who is Never Out of Time

John 11:17, 21 and 32

There are times in life when Jesus seems to be out of time and His presence no longer necessary to our situations. Some of us have lost our hope because we have been praying for something and nothing is coming out. The delays in your life have forced you to think that the presence of Jesus is no longer necessaryy.. It appears as if you are now out of time in terms of being married, passing your O Level, Conceiving, buying a residential stand, getting a sound job, etc. You have been crying to the Lord for many years now but there is no response. This was the case with Mary and Martha. To them the presence of Jesus was no longer necessary. Jesus was now out of time to rescue their brother Lazarus from death. He was now four days late and His presence was no longer necessary. This is why they are saying, 'if you were here .....' In other words they were saying your time to be relevant is over.

Friends in Christ, i want to encourage someone who is in this same situation. Everything in your life appear to be out of time. Everyone of your age is getting married, employed, buying cars, houses, attaining degrees, having children, booming in business, farming, projects etc and you are stuck in one place. Your Lazarus appears to be dead and buried and nothing can reverse that. There is no hope of getting your work permit, Visa, Driver's license, a good job, etc. To you Jesus is four days late and He is now out of time. We are told that a word concerning Lazarus' sickness and death was sent to Jesus, but Jesus was nowhere to be found. He actually came four days after the burial and to the family members His presence was no longer necessary.

God's delay is not His denial. Even If He is four days late, He is never out of time. His delay doesn't matter, what matters most is His presence. Of course you are past the marriageable age, you are past the time to conceive, and your children are now dead and buried. Your marriage is now dead and buried and just like Mary and Martha you are now feeling abandoned by Christ. Today I have some good news for you, even if Jesus is four days late, He is still in time. His delay is not his denial. Jesus is always in time and His presence ushers in a new season/ era to your decomposing marriage, health, business, job/career, Relationship etc. So worry not, even if He is four days late, He is still in time and His presence will reverse the wheels of time to your favour. His presence will call forth your dead and buried Lazarus/ job, intelligence, spouse, children etc out of the grave.

Even if He is four days late He is still in time so never
give up.

With Christ Every Disappointment Comes with a Blessing

Genesis 37:23-28; 41:41-43

In life many people are afraid of their enemies and disappointments. Thus we try by all means to get rid of all our enemies and all those who can disappoint us in life. Majority of our prayer points has to do with asking God to get rid of our enemies or disappointments. But one thing for sure is that we need those opposing forces in life because they act as catalysts to our promotion and success and with Christ on our side our enemies will work for our promotion and every disappointment comes with a blessing. In the above texts we are told of Joseph who was hated, pitted and sold as a slave by his own blood brothers. Joseph's brothers were victims of jealous and their jealous led them to devise ways and means of eliminating their own brother. Friends in Christ, you need these jealous brothers/sisters in your family, at your workplace, school, church, community etc who will put you in a pit, and sell you as a slave for you to get to your Egypt which is a strategic position for your promotion. Joseph faced disappointments from his jealous brothers, and he was stripped off his royal jacket, pitted and sold as a slave to Potiphar. Little did his brothers knew that they were positioning Joseph in a strategic position. Joseph needed people who will place him in Egypt the place of his elevation and this was achieved through his jealous brothers. My friend you need those jealous colleagues at your workplace, in Ministry, in business, in your community, school, at your flea/vegetable market etc for you to get into your Egypt (the place of your elevation.) The more jealousy they are the greater the level of my elevation.

In Egypt Joseph was bought by Potiphar and he was promoted to be in charge of all other slaves in Potiphar's house. Every disappointment comes with a blessing. Then comes Potiphar's wife who falsely accused Joseph and Joseph was potted/ imprisoned. Friends don't be afraid of the Potiphar's wives of our time who are busy making false accusations against you at work, in church, family, society, school etc just because you refused to give in to their evil demands, let them fabricate their stories and put your life, marriage, health, business, children, spouse, brother/sister etc in their hot pot/cage/prison. Every disappointment comes with a blessing to those who believe and are called by God's name. You need these accusers who will falsely accuse you for you to be imprisoned and positioned in a place where the palace favour will locate you. Little did Potiphar's wife knew that the prison was a conducive environment for Joseph to be located by the palace favour. Your elevation or upliftment is made possible by your enemies or those whose aim is to disappoint you. You need those with the Pull Him/Her Down degrees PHD, to pull you down, or to throw you in a pit for you to start climbing the ladder to your success. You need those who will shut you out for you to become more popular. There are some people who think that they can eliminate your influence by shutting you out or throwing you out to the periphery of the periphery like the prison, but one thing I know Jesus will never fail you. He will turn the prison to be the rightful place for the palace favour to locate you. We are told that the palace favour located Joseph in the prison, and He was moved from prison to palace. Listen to Pharaoh's declaration upon Joseph, "I hereby put you in charge of the whole land of Egypt" (Genesis 41:41-43). The more my enemies and those who are jealous about my marriage, business, ministry, life, children, job, education, success, etc are trying to pull me down the higher the level of my success. The more my enemies are trying to shut me out, to lock me in, to throw me at the periphery of the periphery the more popular and successful I become. So my friend don't be afraid of their pits, their roasting pots, because this year their jails will turn to be suitable places to attract the palace favour. Every disappointment carries a blessing and amidst all the disappointments you are passing through, don't lose hope they are leading you to the place of your blessings. Believe in Christ and all your accusers who are busy plotting your destruction in their prisons will see you rising from prison to palace. Let their jails be suitable vehicle that will take us to our rightful destiny in Jesus name. With Christ our enemies will work for our own promotion and every disappointment carries a blessing, so worry not when you see your enemies coming to you like a flood, because the bigger the enemy, the bigger the level of my promotion and my elevation.

Aspire to Inspire Before You Expire

Luke 13:6-10

In the above parable we are told that a man had a fig tree planted in his vineyard, but for 3 years he found no fruits in this fig tree. For us to have a clear picture of this parable, we need to look at the following background. Palestinian soil was so shallow that trees were not grown everywhere. Trees were grown wherever there was good soil to grow them. This is the reason why this fig tree was planted in the vineyard and not in the fig plantation. Thus in the above parable the tree occupied a specially favoured position and had more than an average chance to produce fruits, because it was planted where the soil was shallow. This fig tree was not supposed to be in that vineyard because it was like a weed there, but it was given an opportunity to survive. What an honour or special favour? Thus this tree was to prove itself worthy of this favoured position and failure to do so was tantamount to its removal from that favoured position. That's why the owner of the vineyard in the above parable is instructing his servant to cut it away. Some of us like this fig tree are well positioned, or are placed in these special favoured positions at work, in marriages, Ministry, business, society, political parties, at school etc. From a human point of view you don't deserve to be where you are because there are better qualified people who are much better than you, but it's because of God's grace that you are there.

You might be a school Head with a Certificate in Education as your highest qualification leading University graduates, or you might be a holder of a grade 7 certificate as your highest qualification married to a graduate or you might be a leader/ Pastor /Bishop in the Church leading people who are better qualified and talented than you. From a human point of view you don't deserve to be where you are, and you are like a fig tree planted in a vineyard, so you need to prove yourself worthy of that special position. My friend aspire to inspire before you expire. Remember you are in that special favoured position at your workplace, you are in that sound marriage, in that successful business, leadership position in your church, in that company, you are at that good school etc because of God's grace otherwise you don't deserve to be there because you are just like a fig tree planted in the vineyard. So, prove yourself worthy of that favoured place you are occupying. Aspire to inspire others before you expire.

In the above parable this fig tree failed to live according to expectations and the owner of the vineyard instructed his servant to chop it and remove it from that special favoured position. Brothers and Sisters in Christ, we are placed strategically, and we are occupying favoured positions for a purpose, so aspire to inspire others and to make an impact before you expire. Don't just sit and do nothing just like this fig tree. Produce desired results, make an impact otherwise you will become irrelevant in that special favoured position, and you will be treated just like a weed. You are placed strategically to make an impact wherever you are, so aspire to inspire before you expire. Prove yourself worthy of that favoured position you are occupying, and you will aspire to inspire others before you expire. Inspire others and make an impact and you will Prove wrong all those who are treating you like a weed planted in the vineyard wherever you are positioned. In that marriage prove yourself worthy of that special favoured position.

In Christ There is the Gospel of the Second Chance

Luke 13:6-9

In the above parable, the owner of the field asked his servant to cut the fig tree down because of its unfruitfulness and the Servant said, 'let's give it another year.' In other words, the Keeper is saying lets defer the judgement, I will dig around it and fertilize, and maybe it will produce next time, if it doesn't then chop it down. A fig tree usually takes 3 years to mature and if it's not fruiting by that time it is not likely to fruit. This was the same case with this fig tree, but the Owner allowed it to be given a second chance. Friends, in Christ there is the gospel of the second chance or in Christ judgement is deferred and condemnation is the last resort. Human beings are quick to condemn and most of us have condemned other people, our relatives, colleagues, and have labeled them useless. But it is always Jesus' way to give a person another chance. Of course you have failed to produce the desired results at school, in marriage, in business, at work, in Ministry, in your family etc but that doesn't mean that you are useless, and you can't do anything. You deserve a second chance. This parable teaches us that people rush to condemn and pass judgement on others when they have failed. Human beings are characterized by the gospel of condemnation and elimination like what the story of that woman in John 8:1-11 who was about to be stoned to death.

Human beings are experts in condemning and eliminating others. Make a slight mistake and you are condemned or eliminated. We are quick to condemn and eliminate. Our gospel as humanity is 'Cut it down, why wasting good ground with it any longer.' But Jesus preaches the gospel of the second chance. As we are journeying towards the cross this Lenten period, Christ is saying to all those who have failed in life, you deserve another chance, and your judgement is deferred. Your relatives, Boss, Colleagues at work, in Ministry, at school, your Pastor or Church mates etc have condemned you because you have failed to produce desired results and you are about to be chopped off or eliminated, worry not my friend but believe in Jesus because in him judgement is deferred and there is a gospel of the second chance. To Jesus failure doesn't mean that you are a hopeless and useless case, but it does mean that you need a second chance, and you can make it. Some of us have been condemned to death by our parents, spouses, partners, neighbours, bosses at work, school or in church, in our political parties etc. Others have been eliminated and others are about to be eliminated from their jobs, marriages etc, others are about to be stoned to death and are worried about their future. My friend listen to me and listen well, in Jesus there is the gospel of the second chance and judgement is deferred. Of course you have failed your O level, your diploma, degree, you have failed in business, in marriage etc but you deserve another chance. Jesus is infinitely kind to the person who falls and rises again. Yes you are a sinner par excellence, but you deserve another chance. In this Lenten period Jesus is offering you another chance. Grab the opportunity and produce fruits in Jesus name.

With Christ our Empty Situations Become Full

John 2:1-10

In the Jewish custom the groom was supposed to provide enough food and wine for all the guests in attendance of one's wedding ceremony and to provide inadequate wine was a humiliating experience on the part of the groom. In the above wedding we are told that there was shortage of wine, and the situation was desperate. The wedding was empty of wine but thank God Jesus was among the special Guests who were invited to this wedding. Jesus was not there by accident, but he was invited. Friends in Christ you need to take Jesus as your special Guest and your empty situation will be full. When the situation becomes empty, barren, desperate, the presence of Christ will make a difference. When the wedding was empty of wine, his friends and other invitees could do nothing to rescue the situation and others began to laugh at the groom and calling him all sorts of humiliating names, but the presence of Jesus made a difference. We are told that Jesus asked the people to fill the 6 empty jars with water. The number 6 here is symbolic, it means empty, incomplete, inadequate and imperfect situation, this is why I am saying With

Christ your empty Situation becomes full. When the situation becomes empty or inadequate the presence of Christ will make a difference.

Friends in Christ, there are times when life becomes empty or dry. Some of us are experiencing this emptiness in our marriages, relationships, in business, spiritually, etc. Take Jesus as your special Guest and your empty marriage, which is now empty of true love, true peace, true joy, etc will be refilled with sweet wine. In your inadequate, dry, barren and desperate situation, the presence of Christ will make a difference. Of course you are experiencing this emptiness in your business and nothing meaningful is coming out of that business of yours, no meaningful salary is coming from your work, flea or vegetable market and the situation is really desperate. You need Jesus the one who can refill your empty situation. Jesus instead of joining those who were now mocking the groom, took action and provided the wine. Brothers and Sisters in Christ an empty situation calls us for action and not more words. When others were busy describing the magnitude of the crisis, Jesus took action and he provided that scarce resource. This is the mind of a true believer. We have our beloved friends, relatives, neighbours or fellow Zimbabweans whose situations are empty of food, clothes, good health, shelter, etc because of cyclone and the situation is desperate.

In the above text Jesus showed us that we need to take action. His presence changed things for the better. So you need Christ, and your empty and inadequate situation will be full. Jesus is gonna change that empty situation of yours, of your children, spouse, relative, neighbour etc and what you just need to do is to make sure that he is present in your life. With Christ you will have sweet wine from the beginning to the end. So take Jesus as your special Guest in your life, marriage, at your workplace, relationship etc and that empty situation of yours will become full. With Christ every empty, inadequate, incomplete situation will be full, and every dry, barren and desperate situation will be fruitful. So worry not but focus on Christ and He will turn your mourning into dancing. To all the victims of the Cyclones, wars etc who are experiencing emptiness in everything, we pray that Christ will refill all your empty jars in Jesus name. In that empty and desperate situation focus on Christ the only one who can refill your empty situations. As Christians let's remember that we are Christ's hands thus there is need for us to take the role of Christ and help in refilling the empty jars of those whose lives are empty of basic needs and spiritual needs. With Christ all our human emptiness will be full of extraordinary and sweet wine. Remember to fill someone's empty jar today.

Pursue a Life of Grace Despite your Barren Situation

Samuel 1:1-8 and 2:1-8

For us to have a clear understanding of the above topic, we need to define the word Hannah first. The word Hannah means sufficient Grace. The bible tells us that Hannah was barren and Peninah used to mock her because of her barrenness. Look at this contradiction here, the person whose name suggests a life of sufficient grace was in actual fact associated with a curse. In these days barrenness was associated with a cursed life. Thus Hannah lived a life that was a complete contradiction of her name. Instead of enjoying the sufficient grace as her name suggests, Hannah lived a cursed life characterized by mockery from Peninah. Of course the barren condition was there but it was temporary because sufficient grace was Hannah's portion. My friends in Christ, are you aware that barrenness is not our portion, we are destined for sufficient grace so never allow barrenness to take a permanent position in your life. Pursue this sufficient grace despite that barren situation you are in. I like Hannah's character in the above text, she refused to allow barrenness to overshadow the grace of God upon her life. Hannah continued to pursue a life of grace despite being surrounded by barrenness. Barrenness means a condition of deprivation and lack, an unfruitful and dry situation. So we are saying God's grace is sufficient despite that condition of deprivation and lack or the unfruitful and dry situation you are in.

Of course barrenness, unfruitfulness or lack may appear to be dominating your life, marriage, ministry, business etc but don't be discouraged because no amount of barrenness can overshadow the grace of God upon your life. Barrenness is not your portion, but you are destined for a life full of grace. Worry not my friend when life appears to be barren, remember God's grace is still sufficient even if you are surrounded by conditions of lack, deprivation. Pursue a life of grace despite your barren situation. Hannah/ sufficient grace is your name and not barrenness. Brethren let's pursue a life of grace despite all these conditions of deprivation and lack surrounding us. Poverty is not our portion, destitution is not our portion, unsuccessful careers, businesses, projects, relationships etc are not our portions. We are destined for our Samuel and our Samuel is coming. What you only need to do is to pursue a life of grace in that contrary environment. Be like Hannah the woman who pursued her grace in an environment surrounded by barrenness.

Hannah proved that Grace is stronger than a Curse and no amount of curse can overshadow the grace of God upon your life. So don't worry about the Peninnah's of this life who are busy mocking you and calling you names because of your condition of deprivation you are in right now, this is just but a temporal setback meant to make you lose hope so that you will not receive your Samuel. God's grace is sufficient despite that barren situation you are facing right now, so pursue a life of grace. Hannah continued to pray for grace despite her contrary situation and she gave birth to Samuel. Hannah needed only one Son to silence Peninah who had many children. The birth of Samuel overshadowed Peninah and her children and up to now we don't even know the names of Peninnah's children. Hannah is your name hence you are destined for a life of sufficient grace. Despite our barren situation we are facing right now in this country especially after the covid-19 disaster, God's grace is still sufficient. Continue to hope in the Lord and all these conditions of lack, deprivation, destitution, poverty, sickness etc shall expire and you shall receive your Samuel. Friends, we are destined for a life of sufficient grace and barrenness, or all conditions of deprivation are not our portions.

Release My Heel, I Want to Advance to my Portion

Genesis 25:24-26

The above text is one of the most interesting text. It tells us about the birth of Jacob and Esau, and circumstances that influenced their names. The battle begins in verse 22 where we are told that 'the two unborn babies jostled each other within Rebekah's womb. 'Jacob got hold of or grabbed Esau's heel. This means that Esau's future was grabbed beforehand. Are you aware that some of the problems you are facing today began when you were still in your mother's womb. In verse 24 we are told that Esau was the first to come out and he was red and hairy thus he was named Esau which means hairy. Then his brother came out second with his hand grasping/ holding or grabbing Esau's heel and he was named Jacob which means grabber, deceiver, supplanter, crook. In other words Jacob was born a grabber and Esau's future was grabbed by Jacob before birth. Beware of the heel grabbers.

To hold or grab someone's heel is the same as to follow at somebody's heels or to chase closely. It can also mean trying to stop someone or something from coming out completely. Beware of the heel grabbers. Esau's greatest mistake from the start was to allow Jacob to grab his heel. Never allow the devil, your enemies, rivals, etc to get hold of your heel. We are the unstoppable generation so never allow the heel grabbers to stop you from advancing to your portion, from coming out completely and to chase you or monitoring your progress closely. Friends in Christ we are living in a world, nation, community, families, Churches where we are surrounded by these Jacobs/ Heel grabbers. These are the people, spirits whose agenda is to stop us from coming out completely, snatch our rightful portion, stop our progress academically, financially, materially and spiritually.

Later we see Esau's portions being grabbed by his younger brother. First was his birthright and second was his father's deathbed blessings. That spirit of stagnation, which is causing your business, life to be stagnant at one place is as a result of heel grabbers. So never allow anyone or anything to grab your heel. We command all heel Grabbers grabbing the heels of our spirits, children, marriages, brains, churches, relationships, businesses, projects, work, etc to release our heels in Jesus name. Fire upon every hand grabbing my Heel in Jesus name. My time to unleash my hidden Hero/Heroine is now and no heel grabber will stand in my way. I command the devil to release my heel in Jesus name. With Christ on my side I am unstoppable, and no Heel Grabber will succeed. I am destined to advance to my rightful portion, and no one will stop me, not even your evil covenants, witchcraft grabbing my fruitfulness, success in school, business, Ministry, my promotion, sound marriage, relationship, health etc will stop me from coming out completely and advance. This time i will advance in the presence of my Heel Grabbers in Jesus name.

Believe in Christ the Chain Breaker

Acts 12:6-7

In the above text we are told that Peter was sleeping between two soldiers bound with two chains; and the keepers before the prison door kept the prison locked. Then the Angel of the Lord came upon him, and a light shined in the prison, and he smote Peter on the side and raised him up saying, arise up quickly and his chains fell off from his hands. Note that the presence of Christ in the prison drove away all the prison darkness and broke the chains. Peter was in a terrible situation and was awaiting his death. Four sets with four soldiers each were assigned to guard and monitor him. Door keepers were tightly monitoring the locked door to ensure that there is no escape. It was difficult to rescue Peter from this prison either by bribery or stealth. Friends in Christ, some of us are in this same situation, we have been imprisoned and locked in the devil's prisons and the devil has assigned his prison guards and door keepers to monitor us and they are keeping every door closed. Our marriages, health, finances, children, spouses, brothers/sisters, ministries, churches, projects, education etc are bound with chains and are locked in prisons.

Looking with our naked eyes there is no hope of coming out from those prisons and we are at our hope's end. You are lying and feeling useless in their prison waiting for them to end your career, job, marriage, relationship, business, etc. In that hopeless situation believe in Christ The Key and Chain Breaker. In Christ there is breaking of Padlocks and Chains. We are told that night believers were gathered in the upper room praying for Peter. My friends there is power in intercession prayers. Never lose hope even if the situation is now hopeless. Believe in the key and chain breaking God and He will descend into that prison, cage, lion's den, furnace you are locked in. We are told that at midnight the Angel of the Lord descended upon the prison and drove away all the darkness from the prison. With Christ we will never walk in darkness. With God darkness will give way to light and with him we will not escape in darkness, but we will walk out of their prisons, cages, furnaces etc in the light of God.

After driving away all the darkness, all the chains binding Peter broke and fell down and Peter got his total freedom whist in jail. He began to enjoy his freedom in their prison. Heeeey! I like this Chain breaking God to descend upon that prison caging my health, finances, fertility, career, education etc and i pronounce a sudden release and breaking of the devil's chains of antimarriage, barrenness, failure, antiprogress etc in Jesus name. We are calling upon

Angels in the department of chain breaking and door opening to visit you in that prison you are in and this time the devil and his agents will be surprised to see their chains broken, to see us passing through their soldiers guarding us and to see their keys breaking and their doors opening before their eyes. We declare the breaking of every padlock that is locking you in that prison of poverty in Jesus name. Declare that it's your season to receive your total freedom and no key, chain, nor guard or door keeper will stop you from coming out of that prison you are in. In Christ there is breaking of padlocks and Chains. Believe in this Chain Breaker and all chains of poverty, sickness, miscarriage, barrenness, unemployment, antimarriage, failure, misfortunes etc will be broken. Believe in Christ the Key Breaker and every padlock or key locking your life in that prison will be broken and all closed doors of opportunities in terms of scholarships, business, promotions, jobs, etc will be opened for you in Jesus name.

When the Storm is Contrary Focus On Christ/the Storm Rider

Matthew 14:22-32

After the feeding of the multitude Jesus instructed his disciples to crossover to the other side of the lake, while he went up to the mountain to pray. When the disciples had set out back across the lake; one of the sudden storms, for which the lake was notorious, came down. The wind was contrary, and they were struggling against the winds and the waves. Friends in Christ, contrary winds are rising against our lives day in day out. Contrary winds are opposing forces meant to drown or to run over our lives. Contrary forces are rising against us from all angles. Opposing forces coming from our neighbours, in laws, parents, children, workmates, churchmates, relatives, schoolmates, etc are rising against your life and you are now in a desperate situation, and you are starting to sink. When things are quite promising, contrary forces will rise against you. When the disciples were busy struggling with the contrary forces of the lake, Jesus came walking over the storm and its waves. Instead of being drowned by the contrary waves,

Jesus walked over the waves. When the disciples were drowning, they saw Jesus walking over the waves and Peter asked Jesus to give him permission to walk over the waves and permission was granted.

The greek word which is used in verse 25 and 28 for 'in the water' is 'epi te`n thalassan' which means OVER THE WATER. Thus Jesus came to the troubled disciples riding or walking over the water and Peter was given permission to ride the water. We are told that when Peter's focus was on Christ he rode the storm and its dangerous waves. This is why we are saying, when the wind is contrary, focus on Christ and you will become the Storm Rider. When the storms of life rise against your life, education, business etc focus on Christ and you will become the Storm rider. A storm rider is a person who refuses to be drowned but one who is always above the waves. When Peter shifted his focus from Christ he began to sink. Remain focused on Christ and you will ride those contrary waves rising against your ministry, relationship, children etc. Tap the anointing of a Storm Rider and you can ride or walk over all the storms rising against your family, nation, church, business, job, health, etc in Jesus name. With the Resurrection power vested in us we speak 'The Storm Rider favour' to rest upon your life in Jesus name. Jesus our Master rode over all contrary forces including death and he subdued all contrary waves under his feet, so focus on Jesus the Great Storm

Rider and you will become a Storm Rider. In a nation, family, Church, society, etc where contrary storms and waves are now the order of the day, focus on Christ and you will ride every storm coming your way.

With Christ all your Accusers will be Reduced to Stammers and Stutters

Luke 21:12-1

In the above text, Jesus is warning his followers to be mindful of the doomsday Deceivers and the way they will persecute, torture, raise false accusations against all those who believe in Jesus. Jesus is warning his followers of the risks associated with following him. The time will come when everyone will be targeting the throats of all those who carry the name of Christ. He also said that others will end up on the witness stand in courts for no apparent reason but worry not because Christ will give you the words and wisdom that will reduce all your accusers to Stammers and Stutters. Friends in Christ, being faithful to Christ and standing for the truth will invite persecution, false allegations/ accusations, death etc, but it is a sheer evidence of history that the great Christians enjoyed sweet times with Christ when their bodies were in torture and when they were awaiting death. With Christ on your side, a prison can be turned into a palace, a scaffold can be like a throne and the storms of life can be like summer weather.

Everyone including your own relatives, friends, mates, colleagues, neighbours, church mates etc are turning against you and false accusations have been raised against you just because you carry the name of Christ. In such a situation believe in Jesus and He will reduce all your accusers to stammers and Stutters. Your enemies who are threatened by the presence of Jesus in your life, may threaten you with death, dismissal from work, divorce, demotion, barrenness, etc but fear not because we worship a God who will reduce all our accusers to Stammers and Stutters. The person who walks with Christ may lose the campaign but can never lose the battle. We pray that this time our God will reduce our enemies, accusers and all those planning evil against us to Stammers and Stutters and that He will turn their prisons meant to torture us into palaces in Jesus name. Believe in the risen Lord and He will reduce all your accusers to Stammers and Stutters in Jesus name.

Unleashing Stinging Bees and Lighting upon the Enemy's Army

Judges 4:1-15

In the above story we are told that Israel did evil in the sight of the Lord after Ehud's death, and they were put into the hand of Jabin the King of Canaan whose army Commander was Sisera. Jabin had 900 chariots of iron and he mightily oppressed the Children of Israel for 20 years. Then God appointed Deborah to be a Prophetess and judge of Israel. Deborah had his army Commander called Barak. She instructed Barak to go and wage a war against the mighty army of Jabin whose Commander was Sisera. Barak refused to go to war without the company of Deborah, and Deborah rose and went up with him. We are told that the Lord discomfited Sisera and his mighty chariots and Sisera lighted down of his chariot and fled away on his feet. The name Deborah means a 'stinging bee' and the name Barak means 'lightning/ Thunder.' So the army of the people of God was being led by a Stinging Bee and Lightning. That's why we are saying, you have to unleash stinging bees and Lightning upon your enemy's camp.

Let there be stinging bees and Lightning all over the forces of our enemies in Jesus name. Sisera and his mighty forces have been oppressing you and your life is in captivity. The devil has captured your marriage, brains, spirit, children, business, building project, ministry, career, etc and he/she is running all over your life. You are so terrified of your enemies, and you are being tortured left, right and center. Believe in the risen Lord and you will unleash stinging bees and Lightning upon your enemy's camp. In the above text, it was Sisera's mighty army versus stinging bees and Lightning. This time your Sisera has to flee by foot. By the Resurrection Power vested in us we unleash stinging bees and Lightning upon the camp of all witches, Satanist, anti-progress spirits, Jezebel spirits, evil forces etc targeting my life, my children, brothers/sisters etc in Jesus name. Don't run away from your Sisera, remember you are a stinging bee and Lightning. Sting your Sisera and his mighty army and force him to flee by foot. Speak thunder and Lightning upon all evil forces of the devil capturing your life in Jesus name. Be a stinging bee and sting the devil and his army to death in Jesus name. Fear not their mighty chariots, because you have the anointing of a bee and Lightning.

The Presence of Christ will Shake the Devil's Territory

Mark 4:35-41

The above miracle is a nature miracle, and it shows us that Jesus is the Master of everything including nature. In Luke and other synoptic gospels miracles are called Dunamis and they portray the dynamite power or the Mighty/ powerful deeds of Christ. For us to have a clear picture of the above topic, the following background is of paramount importance. Jews believed that when there was a storm at sea, the demons or marine spirits in the sea would have been threatened thus they became violent and needed to be overcome. We are told that when Jesus and his disciples got into the sea, the waters were still and peaceful. We are also told that there were other small boats in that same sea but the boat with Jesus was the target. Thus the presence of Christ in that sea threatened the marine/water spirits who were in charge of that sea. My friend you are being targeted by your colleagues at work, at school, in ministry, in business etc because of Christ in you. You are being targeted by the whole family, your in laws, relatives, neighbours, community witches, satanists etc because of Christ in you.

The presence of Christ in your life is threatening and shaking the devil's territory and strongholds wherever you are. Know that a fruitful tree invites stone throwers and vice versa. If you are moving with Christ, strongholds, principalities, satanic bases etc will tremble and fall. The storm and its waves rose against the boat which was carrying Jesus and we are not told about all other small boats in that same sea being affected by the storm. Friend are you aware that if you are a child of God you will threaten and shake the devil's territory wherever you go, so expect to encounter opposition, storms and waves. If you are a child of God and you are married to a family characterized by witchcraft, be prepared to be hated by your in laws because the Christ in you will threaten and shake their witchcraft base, their satanic powers, their juju etc. The presence of Christ in the sea threatened and shook the base of marine spirits and these spirits tried to counterattack Jesus by raising its waves against him. Those who live and move with Christ in most cases encounter opposition, fierce storms, persecution etc from their mates, neighbours, in laws, bosses, satanists, witches, etc.

Storms have been rising against your marriage, health, family, church, business, multiplication, relationship, education, career, etc and you are questioning God 'why me?' The answer is you have Jesus. The Jesus in you is wreaking havoc in the devil's territory and they are now trying to revenge so worry not because the one in you is greater than thousands of marine spirits responsible for steering the sea and causing the waves to rise against your life and family. Jesus has the dynamite power/Dunamis, and He is The Master of everything including storms, thunder, water spirits, vengeance spirits, alien spirits, satanic spirits, antiprogress spirits, antimarriage spirits, etc, so He will take charge of the situation wherever He is. This is why Jesus was fast asleep on the cushion when the disciples were now in a panic mode. Jesus was in control of the boat because He was sleeping on the driver's seat. So why worry, fear not all those evil forces who rising against your job, health, fertility, project, musika, education, career etc, the presence of Jesus in your life is shaking the devil's base and stronghold.

With Christ your Destination is Guaranteed

Mark 4:35-41

In the above text Jesus is telling his Disciples of the next move, LET US CROSS OVER.... This statement means that Jesus is the initiator or author of the journey, and He is part of the plan thus He will take you to the other side come what may. The words Cross Over means the way to the other side is already designed and your rightful destination is guaranteed. We are told that, when they got into the sea the storm tossed their boat left, right and center and the disciples went into a panic mode. They tried to save themselves forgetting that Jesus the initiator and author of the Journey was present. Instead of allowing Jesus to take them to the other side the disciples tried to take Jesus to the other side and their journey was disastrous. Jesus was fast asleep on a cushion/stern. This was the driver's seat thus Jesus was on the steering and in control of the boat, but the disciples failed to notice that, and they tried to put the matter in their own hands.

The storm and its accompanying waves became a barrier meant to stop Jesus and the disciples from reaching their rightful destiny. This is the main agenda of the devil and his agents. They don't want us to reach our rightful destiny in life so they will fight us and raise storms against us so as to force us to divert from our goals. But with Christ on our side our rightful destination is guaranteed. What you just need to do is to leave everything in his hands. Don't try to use your experience like what the disciples did. The more they tried to save themselves using their experience, the more the water filled the boat. It was only after realizing that Christ is the author of the journey that they were saved. Brethren, Christ has already designed the way for us to crossover to a better future, better jobs, sound marriages, fruitful businesses etc but there are some obstacles that will arise so as to stop us, divert us so that we will not reach our rightful destinations. Storms may rise against your marriage, relationship, health, family, business, education, job, ministry etc but Christ will not leave you halfway. With him in your boat your rightful destination is guaranteed. No matter what obstacles i will crossover to my rightful destiny. I am not destined to a halfway destination. Even if the enemy comes to me like a flood I am guaranteed of a safe passage to my rightful destiny. With Christ on my side No storm, no wave, no Giant, no evil force will stop me from reaching my rightful destiny. With Him on my side I am guaranteed of my rightful marriage, my rightful job, relationship, my sound health, successful project, career, ministry, etc in Jesus name.

Your Level of Faith Determines your Challenges

1 Corinthians 10:13

Brothers and Sisters in Christ, temptations do come in life, but there is always a way out. In the above text Paul informs us that our level of faith determines our temptations. High level people in terms of faith face high level challenges and temptations are inevitable in this life. Dogs never bark at a parked car and a tree with fruits attracts stone throwers. In the above text Paul is certain that temptations and challenges will come, it is part of the essence of Christian life but one thing for sure is that no temptation/ challenge is unique. Others have experienced it, endured it and have come through it. The word temptation in the above text means something which is designed, not to make you fall, but to test you, so that you will emerge from it stronger than ever. In verse 13 Paul says, "for every temptation there is always a way out." Here Paul used the Greek word *ekbasis* which means 'a way out of a defile, a mountain pass and this refers to an army apparently surrounded by its enemies and then suddenly seeing an escape route to safety. This is why we are saying your level determines your temptations or challenges.

Temptations are like steps of a ladder, each time you overcome them you go to the next level, and you will become stronger than before. Everything that God allows you to go through he knows that you have the capacity to withstand. This is why Paul says we are hard pressed, but we are not hemmed. Your level determines your Temptations or challenges. As Christians be prepared to face temptations and challenges. It's not a sin to be tempted but no person need fall to any temptation, because for every temptation there is always ekbasis/ a way out or an escape route to safety. So never allow the devil to put you in tight a corner that you will fail to find the escape route. God will not allow you to be tested beyond what you are able to bear. Your level determines the nature of your challenges and temptations. So don't give in to those temptations coming your way, there is always an escape route, and the way out is not the way of surrender, and not the way of retreat, but it is the way of conquest in the power of the grace of God.

In most cases when people are tempted they fail to see the escape route, but the ekbasis/way out is there always. My friend, are you about to give in to the temptations or challenges you are facing in your marriage, at your workplace, in your family, Church, school etc? Are you about to surrender because the pressure from those temptations and challenges is becoming unbearable and you are now feeling drained, exhausted, defeated? As we are moving in this Christian journey know that your level of faith determines your challenges, High level people in terms of faith encounter high level temptations and challenges, so ask God to give you the power to rise above every temptation. Remember that for every temptation no matter how big and frightening it is, there is always ekbasis/a way out. When you face temptations and challenges know that you have the capacity to conquer them so ask God to show you this ekbasis/ a way out or an escape route to your safety. Those challenges and temptations you are facing in your family, marriage, ministry, at your workplace, school, in business etc God knows that you have the capacity to withstand, and He knows that there is always a way out.

With Christ your Absence will Stop all the Proceedings

1 Samuel 16:11-13

In the above text Samuel is send by God to anoint another King following King Saul's disobedience. The anointing was to be done without the knowledge of Saul and it was to be done upon one of the sons of Jesse. Then Jesse called out all his sons to come to this event, but David was forgotten. Jesse would remember David when it comes to issues of tending the sheep, but on issues of anointing and feasting, David was forgotten. In life there are some people who will remember you only when they want to benefit from you, and they don't even care about you when things are good. They want you to tend their sheep, but they don't want you to be in the Blessing zone. They associate you with a Shepherd who is not fit to be blessed. This was Jesse's mentality, instead of bringing all his sons to the anointing/ blessing zone, he left out David.

By the way the name David means the Beloved one of God. So Jesse left the Beloved one of God out and he invited a heap of unfavored people at the anointing table. Is the beloved/ favoured one of God in your midst? Someone is missing at your table. Friends in Christ, it's a sheer waste of time to gather without the beloved/ favoured one of God in your midst. Listen to Samuel's question when he realized that Jesse had brought a bunch of unanointable people before him, "Are these all the sons you have?" Heeeey! Someone is missing here. The rightful person is missing. Friends worry not when you see your colleagues, family members, Bosses, neighbors, etc sidelining you. You have been left out and forgotten in terms of promotion at work, in church etc and they are busy surrounding themselves with those who appears to be fit for the posts in their eyes but in God's eyes they are not fit. They only think about you when they want to use you.

This time you will not sit down to eat my portion. Listen to Jesse's reply, "There is still the youngest, but he's out in the fields watching the sheep and goats." This response shows us that Jesse was not even counting David as the anointable material. But Samuel instructed Jesse to call David and He declares that "we will not sit down to eat until he arrives." I love this verse. Let them isolate you, let them gather to feast in your absence, this time no one is going to sit at the table of my blessings without my permission. Noone is going to feast in my abscence. You have been disqualified by people on many occasion but this time your absence will stop the proceedings. My abscence will stop every proceeding. Someone is missing here. With Christ on your side your absence will stop all the proceedings. Believe in Jesus and grace will locate you even if you are forgotten.

With Christ no Hacker will Succeed.

Daniel 10:12-13

To Hack into means to gain unauthorized access to a network, or online account belonging to a person or organization by manipulating code.[6]Hackers are those people who specialize in Hacking. The devil's main agenda is to hack into the secret of your success through manipulating the password of your joy and favour. This was the business of the Persian Kings. We are told that, God heard and responded to Daniel's pleas on the very first day. But the Prince of the kingdom of Persia HACKED into or gained unauthorized entry into Daniel's network or online account and hijacked Daniel's blessings for 21 days. Every Christian has His/her online account. When praying, one uses his/her online account and his/her own password to get to the father who is our God. The business of the devil or our enemy is to gain unauthorized entry into our online account by manipulating our password. Such were the Persian Kings. They Hacked into Daniel's online account and they hijacked his blessing and delayed him for three weeks.

Then God did send the Angel Michael to go and deal with the Hackers of Daniel's blessings. My friend, the devil has gained unauthorized entry into your online account and has manipulated the password to the secret of your success, joy and favour. Your enemy has hijacked your Blessings and you have been delayed in so many ways, both physically, spiritually and materially. The Persian Kings within your family, community, workplace, Church, school, marketplace etc have gained access into your network and they are busy delaying you from conceiving, multiplying, excelling in school, in ministry, business, etc. But one thing for sure is that God send his only begotten Son, Jesus Christ whose resurrection power rendered the blessing hackers powerless and useless. Thus believing in this Risen Christ would render all our blessing hackers useless and powerless. With the resurrection power vested in us we declare that from today onwards, no Hacker will gain unauthorized entry into the secret of your success. All your enemies who used to manipulate the password to your joy, peace, sound marriage, promotion, success, good health etc will not succeed in Jesus name. With Christ on our side no Hacker will succeed in manipulating the password to our Blessings. We command every Persian king or the Hackers of our time, to get out of our online account for good in Jesus name

Beware of Dream/Vision Killers

Genesis 37:5-11and19-20

Joseph was a man of dreams/visions, and he was born a dreamer. Proverbs 29:18a says, "where there is no vision people perish." This means that for one to become a winner/ champion in life one needs to have a deep and fixed sense of vision or be a dreamer. A vision is a clear picture of the future that you desire, or you are moving towards. For you to achieve your greatness in life you need to pursue your dreams or your vision. Joseph shared his dreams with his family members, and he was expecting them to support him fulfilling his dreams, but the opposite was true. Instead of helping him to achieve his dreams his brothers became jealous, and they hatched a plan to kill Joseph's dreams. Friends in Christ when you start to do something about your dreams or vision bear in mind that your situation will not be friendly and inviting. Be prepared to encounter opposition from those whom you think will support you. In Joseph's case his own blood brothers became obstacles or his dream killers. In most cases those who are irritated by your talent and those who want to kill your vision are those who are very close to you and those who are supposed to help you achieve your dreams, like your family members, relatives, workmates, schoolmates, churchmates, neighbours etc.

The bible tells us that, the more Joseph told his brothers about his dreams the more his brothers hated him. Despite this hatred from his dream killers Joseph continued to dream big. My friend continue to dream big, think big, see big even in the presence of your dream killers. We are surrounded by dream killers and these dream killers target those with extraordinary dreams. They are not worried about people of ordinary dreams. If you want to invite their anger, start to dream big at your company, in your Church, family, community etc and start to take steps towards your dreams. When Joseph started taking steps towards his dreams, his brothers hated him to death and you can hear from their conversation, "here comes the dreamer, let's kill him and we will see what would become of his DREAMS. Look here, the target was the dreams. Beware of the Dream killers wherever you are and where you go. These people will not rest until they destroyed your dreams or vision.

Pursue your dreams or vision even if dream killers are coming to you like a flood. Be like Martin Luther King jr who continued to dream big in the presence of his Dream Killers and i quote his dreams: "I say to you my friends, that in spite of the difficulties and frustrations of the moment i still have a dream. I have a dream that one day on the red hills of Georgia the sons and daughters of former slaves and the sons and daughters of former slave owners will be able to sit down together at the table of brotherhood. I have a dream that one day the state of Mississippi, a desert sweating in the heart of injustice and oppression, will be transformed into an Oasis of freedom and justice. I have a dream that one day that one day my four little children will live in a nation where they will not be judged by the colour of their skin but by the content of their character......" Luther King jr continued to dream big in the presence of his oppressors and dream killers. My friend pursue your dreams, continue to dream big, aim high, think big, see big even in the presence of your dream Killers. Some of us have failed to achieve big things in life because we were threatened by these Dream Killers at work, in business, in Ministry, at school, in our families etc. Listen my friend and listen well, if you want to be a champion in life pursue your dreams come hail come thunder, take action and start to move towards your dreams. Be a missionary to your vision and never allow Dream Killers to stop you from advancing towards your vision. My brothers and Sisters in Christ, pursue your dreams at whatever cost. Champions continue to dream big even in the presence of their dream Killers. Joseph pursued his dreams and he ended up being a Governor in a foreign land. Continue to dream big, think big and see big even if the situation is desperate because with Christ no dream Killer will stop your greatness.

Our Jesus is Bigger than our Giants

1 Samuel 17:36-37

In the above text we encounter the God who is a Giant Killer. With him on your side Giants will fall, bears, hyenas and the lions targeting your life will fall. Goliath was a giant and a destructive spirit and in terms of stamina all Israelite soldiers trembled upon hearing his voice. For forty days the Israelite army was shut down by one harassing voice. On the fortieth day a kid arrived, and his name was David. The name David means 'The Beloved one of God' and the number 40 represents the period of severe testing and suffering. Thus in the above text, the Israelite army experienced a severe testing, suffering and humiliation from the destructive spirit for 40 days and they were now demoralized and feeling defeated.

For them Goliath was too big to challenge. Then comes a kid who was too small to be noticed by Goliath. There was a slight increase in the Israelite camp. It was just a slight increase, but this slight increase would later change the game. David was not a professional soldier in terms of receiving army training, but he had received Divine training. He was the beloved one of God hence Divine Favour was upon him. With Christ on your side, every giant standing against your life is too big to miss. David had received a more advanced training and his Trainer was God. Listen to his words in the above text, 'The Lord who rescued me from the paw of the lion and the paw of the bear will rescue me from this uncircumcised Philistine.' In other words David was saying my God is Greater than your Giant and his name is Jehovah The Giant Killer. With him on my side Giants will fall. This fight was a first-round knockout, it lasted for 10 seconds, and the destructive spirit was no more.

Friends in Christ we are being tormented day and night by these destructive forces or giants of our time. Giants are tormenting our marriages, bodies, spirits, children, sisters, brothers, etc and we are now feeling defeated, demoralized and helpless. Our Goliath are humiliating us day and night and Goliath is too big to challenge. Take Jesus as your Commander in Chief and you will realize that Goliath is too big to miss. Jesus is The Giant Killer and with him, Giants attacking your life will fall and die in the first round. With Jesus The Giant Killer on your side, Killing your Goliath is as easy as cutting margarine with a hot knife. Your God is greater than all those giants threatening your relationship, marriage, business, ministry, etc. You just need to undergo Divine training and Goliath will fall in Jesus name.

With God behind the Scenes your Destiny is Assured

Genesis 45:1-20

In the above text Joseph is telling his brothers about how God has used their cruelty for his own good. Joseph is reminding his brothers that He is still alive, and that God has used all forms of cruelty done to him as steppingstones to his elevation. The story of Joseph teaches us that with God our destiny is assured come hail, come thunder. His brothers pitted him and later sold him to the Ishmaelites and to them Joseph was now history. Are you aware that you have a destiny, and nothing can stop you from reaching your destiny. Your enemies can try to delay, stop, divert, manipulate you but be assured of this, they cannot terminate what God has generated, cultivated, elevated, appointed and anointed.

Joseph was anointed to be a leader from birth and his brothers became Jealous about him and they devised cruel methods to eliminate him from the scene, but with God behind the scene his destiny was guaranteed. Friends in Christ, it's a sheer waste of time to try and terminate what God has appointed and anointed. Joseph's brothers tried it but here they are, face to face with the person whom they sold as a slave to the Ishmaelites but now He is no longer a Slave but Second in Command or The Governor of Egypt. Listen to Joseph's words to his brothers, 'I am Joseph your brother.....God send me here before you to preserve life.'

His statement implied that his brothers' cruelty against him was God's plan to transport Joseph to Egypt in advance so that He would later save them. Friends in Christ, with God behind the scene, your destiny is assured, so don't be discouraged by your enemies whose aim is to divert, stop or block you from reaching your destiny. Paul says, 'everything works for good to those who believe and to those who are called by his name.' (Romans 8:28) Believe in God and your destiny will be assured. Those who are wishing bad things, those who are planning evil against you today shall bow before you tomorrow. Your relatives, workmates, colleagues, neighbours who are working against your elevation today are going to be the beneficiaries of your elevation. With God behind the scene our destiny is assured, and no evil plot of the devil will stop us from reaching our destiny. Amen.

www.ingramcontent.com/pod-product-compliance
Lightning Source LLC
Chambersburg PA
CBHW031225120626
46545CB00003B/990